THE MAGIC BUS
INSIDE THE HUMAN BODY

By Joanna Cole   Illustrated by Bruce Degen

Kingfisher Books

The author and illustrator wish to thank Dr Arnold J. Capute,
Associate Professor of Pediatrics, Director, Division of Child Development,
Johns Hopkins University of Medicine, for his help in preparing this book.

Kingfisher Books, Grisewood & Dempsey Ltd,
Elsley House, 24–30 Great Titchfield Street,
London W1P 7AD

First published in paperback in the UK in 1991 by Kingfisher Books
10 9 8 7 6 5 4 3 2 1
First published in hardback in the UK in 1990 by Kingfisher Books
Published by arrangement with Scholastic Inc.

BRITISH LIBRARY CATALOGUING-IN-PUBLICATION DATA
Cole, Joanna, *1944–*
Inside the human body
1. Man. Body
I. Title II. Degen, Bruce III. Series
612

ISBN 0 86272 788 X

Printed in Spain

To Craig
from Joanna
& Bruce

It all began when Ms Frizzle
showed our class a filmstrip
about the human body.
We knew trouble was about to start,
because we knew Ms Frizzle
was the strangest teacher in the school.

The very next day, The Friz made us do an experiment on our own bodies.

Then she announced that we were going on a class trip to the science museum. We were going to see an exhibit about how our bodies get energy from the food we eat.

YOUR CELLS NEED ENERGY TO HELP YOU GROW, MOVE, TALK, THINK, AND PLAY.

Jail cell →

JUST BEING IN MS. FRIZZLE'S CLASS TAKES ALL MY ENERGY.

DIFFERENT KINDS OF CELLS HAVE DIFFERENT JOBS
by Gregory

Lung cells help you breathe.

Muscle cells help you move.

ODE TO JELLY

Brain cells help you think.

When it was time to go,
everyone got back on the bus—
everyone but Arnold.
He was still at the picnic table,
daydreaming and eating
a bag of Cheesie-Weesies.

WHEN YOU EAT, YOUR BODY DIGESTS THE FOOD SO YOUR CELLS CAN USE IT TO MAKE ENERGY.

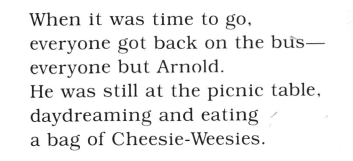

YOUR BODY NEEDS GOOD FOOD
by Carmen
For high energy and good growing power eat lots of:

Fresh fruits and Vegetables

Milk and Milk products

Whole grain cereal and Pasta

CEREAL   BROWN RICE

Lean Meats, Fish, Poultry, AND eggs

AND NOT TOO MUCH JUNK FOOD!

A SCIENCE WORD
by Dorothy Ann

Digestion comes from a word that means to divide. When food is digested it is divided into smaller and smaller parts.

"Hurry up, Arnold!" called Ms Frizzle. She reached for the ignition key, but instead she pushed a strange little button nearby.

At once, we started shrinking and spinning through the air.

From inside, we couldn't see what was happening. All we knew was that we landed suddenly...

and then we were going down a dark tunnel.
We had no idea where we were.
But, as usual, Ms Frizzle knew.
She said we were inside a human body,
going down the oesophagus—
the tube that leads from the throat
to the stomach.
Most of us were too upset
about leaving Arnold behind
to pay much attention.

WHERE'S ARNOLD?

HE GOT LEFT!

THAT'S WHAT HAPPENS WHEN YOU EAT JUNK FOOD!

I THOUGHT WE WERE GOING TO THE MUSEUM.

THERE'S BEEN A SLIGHT CHANGE OF PLANS... WE'RE BEING DIGESTED INSTEAD.

FOOD GOES TO YOUR STOMACH THROUGH THE OESOPHAGUS
by Wanda
The food does not just fall down. It is pushed along by muscle actions the way toothpaste is squeezed out of a tube. That's why you can swallow even when you are upside down.

MUSCLES SQUEEZE TO PUSH FOOD TO YOUR STOMACH

WHY DOES YOUR STOMACH GROWL?
by Phil

Sometimes your stomach churns when there is not much food in it. Then the gases in your stomach make a gurgling sound.

"We are now passing into the stomach,"
said Ms Frizzle.
It wasn't exactly *quiet* in there.
The walls of the stomach moved in and out,
churning and mashing the food
into a thick liquid.
The bus was turning round and round,
and digestive juice splashed the windows.
Now we knew how it felt to be a hamburger!

YOUR STOMACH IS LIKE A BUILT-IN FOOD PROCESSOR.

GURGLE!

ROLL UP YOUR WINDOWS, CHILDREN.

YUCK!

WHY ARE THE INTESTINES COILED UP?
by John
In an adult the intestines are 7.5 metres (25 feet) long. If they were stretched out straight, a person would have to be as tall as a house.

STOMACH

FOOD GOES FROM THE STOMACH TO THE SMALL INTESTINE

WASTE GOES OUT THROUGH THE LARGE INTESTINE

The small intestine was
a coiled-up hollow tube.
The inner walls of the tube were covered
with tiny "fingers" called *villi*.
"In the *villi* are tiny blood vessels.
Food molecules are taken into
these blood vessels,"
said Ms Frizzle.
"Once the food is in the blood,
it can travel all over the body."

We felt ourselves getting even smaller,
and Ms Frizzle started driving
into one of the *villi*.
She was going straight into a blood vessel!

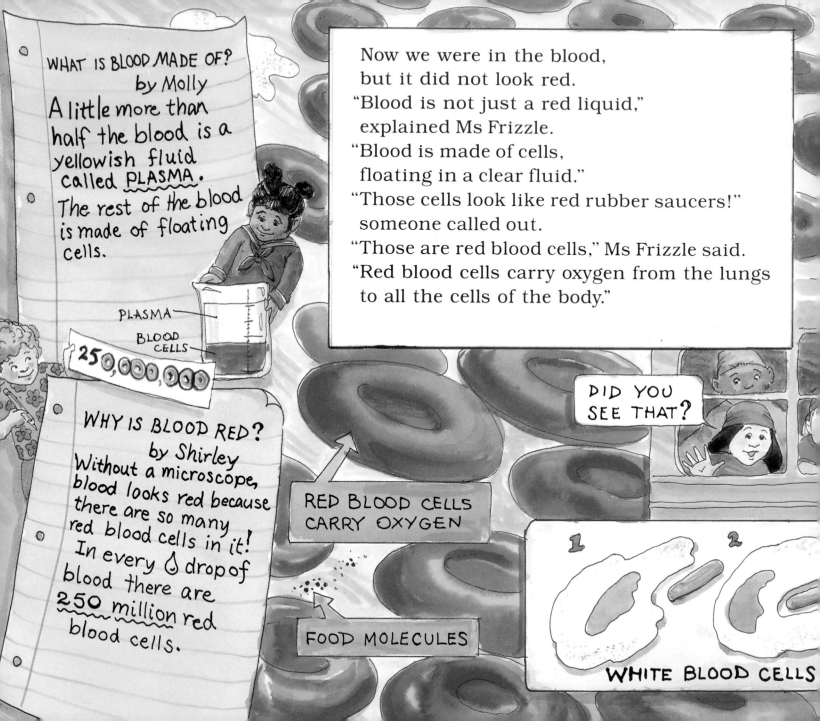

Looking back, we saw a white blood cell
chasing the bus.
"We'll be safer with the red blood cells, kids,"
said Ms Frizzle.
She reached for the handle
that controlled the bus's doors.
"Don't do it!" we cried,
but when did Ms Frizzle ever listen?
The doors of the bus flew open.

THAT WHITE BLOOD
CELL MUST THINK
THE SCHOOL BUS
IS A GERM.

WELL, THE BUS
IS PRETTY DIRTY.

We were swept out of the bus
and into the bloodstream.
"Everybody hitch a ride!" called The Friz.
Each kid grabbed a red blood cell
as it went by.
Our last glimpse of the bus
was when it went into another blood vessel—
with the white blood cell right behind it!

YOUR HEART IS A PUMP
by Florrie

When the walls of the heart chambers squeeze together they pump out blood, just the way you can squeeze water out of a plastic squeeze bottle.

OOPS!

HEY!

Right Lung — Left Lung — Heart

YOUR HEART PUMPS USED BLOOD INTO THE LUNGS TO GET FRESH OXYGEN.

RIGHT LUNG

The next thing we knew, we had flowed into the heart. "Inside the heart are four hollow spaces, called *chambers*," said Ms F. "Each chamber is a little pump." The two chambers on the right side of the heart took in used blood from the body and pumped it to the lungs.

TO THE RIGHT LUNG

USED BLOOD FROM UPPER BODY

1st CHAMBER

2nd CHAMBER

USED BLOOD FROM LOWER BODY

HAVE A HEART, MS FRIZZLE, GET US OUT OF HERE!

BLOOD GOES ROUND
AND ROUND
by Michael
In less than a minute
your blood makes
a trip all around
your body.
This is called the
circulation of the
blood.

ONE MORE SCIENCE WORD
by Dorothy Ann
Circulate comes from
a word that means
"to circle". Blood
circulates - circles -
all around your body.

From the lungs, our red blood cells carried us back to the heart. This time we were on the left side of the heart—the side that pumps fresh blood back to the body again. "Kids, it looks as if these red blood cells are on their way to the brain," said Ms Frizzle.

LOOK! WHEN THE RED BLOOD CELLS PICK UP OXYGEN, THEY TURN BRIGHT RED.

FROM RIGHT LUNG

AIR SAC

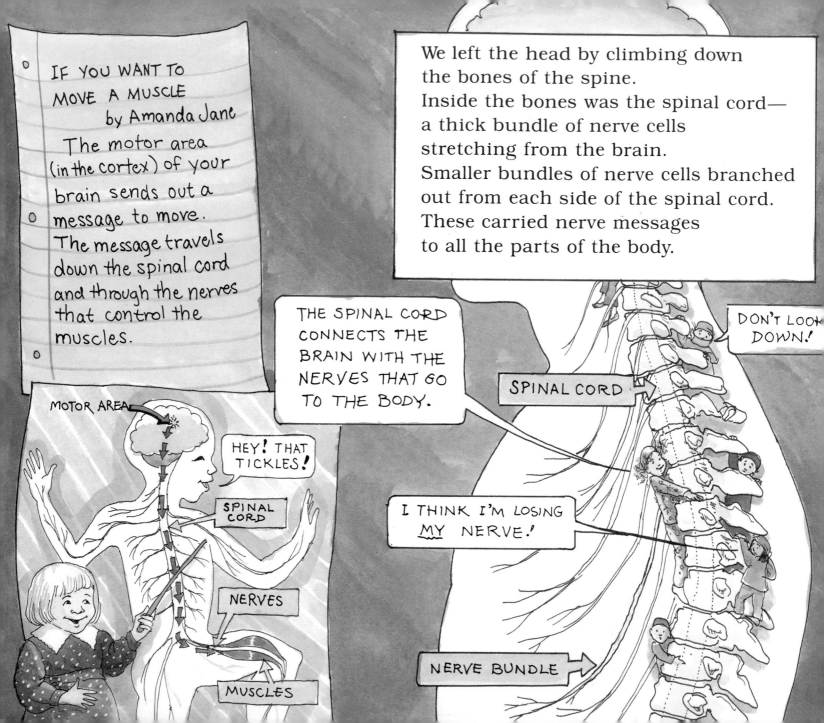

We followed some nerves that went to the leg muscles.
The leg muscles were working hard.
They needed a lot of energy.
They used up a lot of food and oxygen from the blood.
The heart was beating faster to carry fresh blood to the muscle cells.

MUSCLES MOVE YOUR BONES
by Tim
Some muscles are attached to bones. When the muscles contract (get shorter) they pull on the bones. That makes the bones move, and then you more.

MUSCLES
BONES

CHILDREN, WE ARE SLIDING ON A MUSCLE. FROM HERE, WE'LL RETURN TO THE BLOODSTREAM.

NERVE ENDING

MUSCLE FIBRE

I'LL GET THERE SOONER IF I RUN! (PANT! PANT!)

I WONDER WHERE ARNOLD IS NOW.

I HAVE THE STRANGEST FEELING HE'S CLOSE BY.

THE MORE ACTIVE YOU ARE THE FASTER YOUR HEART BEATS.

THUMP THUMP

BLOOD VESSEL

We entered a nearby blood vessel.
The blood was moving so fast,
we were afraid we would
lose each other.
But at that moment,
the school bus floated by.
What a relief!
We jumped on and went up
through the heart and lungs again—
just the way we went before.

CLASS, WE'RE ON THE WAY OUT OF THE BODY.

RELAX, WE'RE GOING BACK NOW.

I CAN'T RELAX AS LONG AS I SEE BLOOD CELLS OUTSIDE THE WINDOW.

When we emerged from the bloodsteam,
we were in a huge open space.
"Where are we?" asked a kid.
Ms Frizzle explained,
"Children, this is the nasal cavity."
"The what?" we asked.
"The inside of the nose," said The Friz.
Suddenly, we heard a deafening noise.
It sounded like "Ah-aa-aa-ah!"

WHAT MAKES YOU SNEEZE?
by Phoebe

If something is tickling the inside of your nose, the tickling signals your brain.

The brain makes you take an extra big breath. (That's when you say Aaah!)

Then your brain makes your chest muscles squeeze your lungs.

Air rushes out at speeds of up to 100 miles per hour. (Thats when you say choo!)

Then we heard, "CHOOOOOO!"

CLASS, THE SOUND YOU HEAR IS A SNEEZE.

ANYTHING IN THE NOSE CAN MAKE YOU SNEEZE. IT COULD BE A BIT OF DIRT OR DUST, OR SOME BACTERIA.

IN THIS CASE IT HAPPENS TO BE A SCHOOL BUS.

A tremendous blast of air
hit the bus full force.
We flew forward,
spinning round and round.

We were going so fast,
we couldn't see anything,
but we could tell we were getting bigger.
Then—thud!—we landed.
There we were, back at school.
And there was Arnold,
in the school car park,
blowing his nose.

WE'RE BACK!

LOOK! THERE'S ARNOLD!

THUD

"Arnold!" we said, "the trip was *amazing!*
You should have been there!"

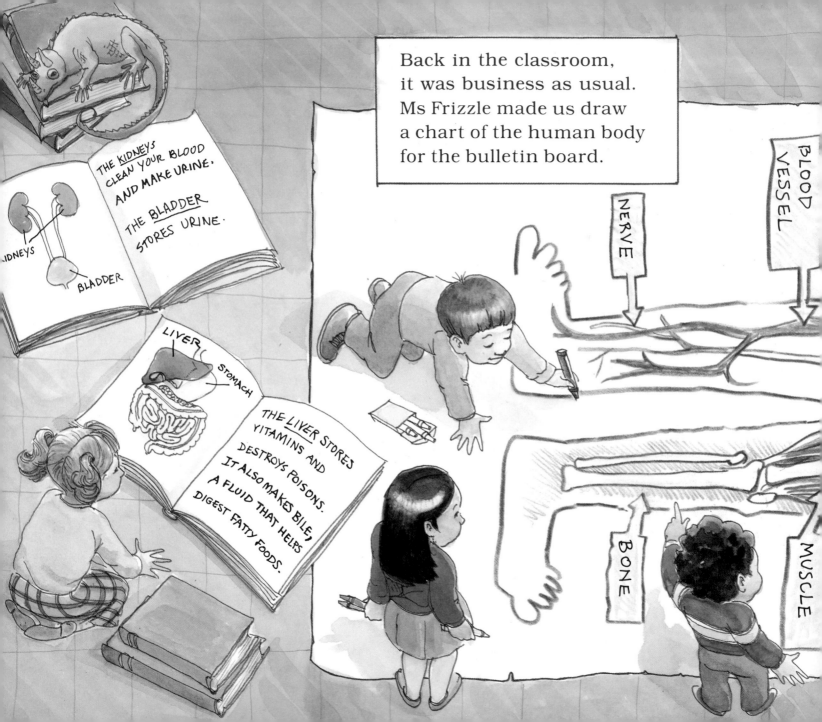

Back in the classroom, it was business as usual. Ms Frizzle made us draw a chart of the human body for the bulletin board.

THE KIDNEYS CLEAN YOUR BLOOD AND MAKE URINE.

THE BLADDER STORES URINE.

KIDNEYS

BLADDER

LIVER

STOMACH

THE LIVER STORES VITAMINS AND DESTROYS POISONS. IT ALSO MAKES BILE, A FLUID THAT HELPS DIGEST FATTY FOODS.

NERVE

BLOOD VESSEL

BONE

MUSCLE

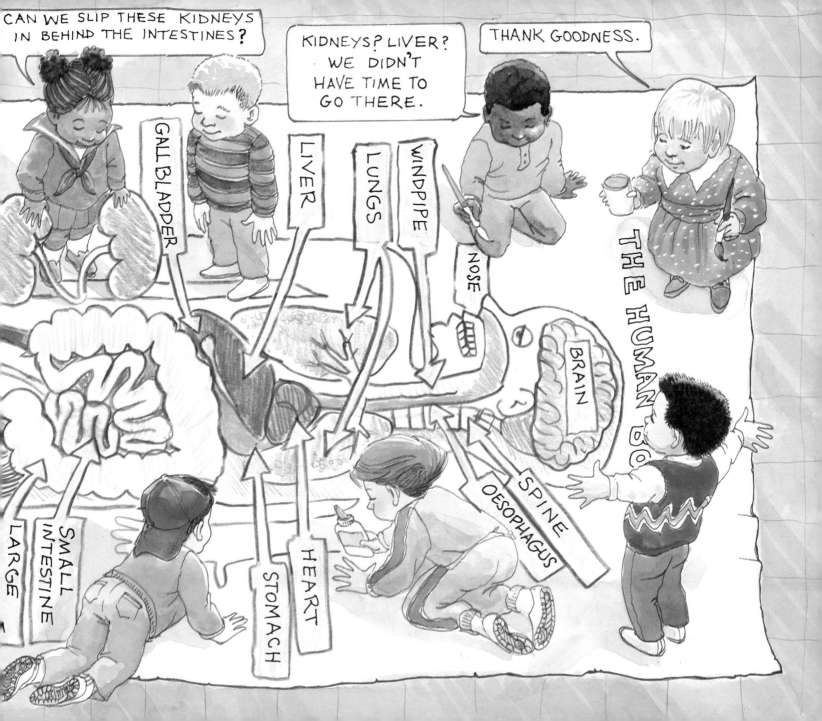

TRUE-OR-FALSE TEST

STOP! TAKE THIS TEST!
DO NOT WATCH T.V. ... YET.
DO NOT GET A SNACK ... YET.
DO NOT PLAY A VIDEO
GAME ... YET.

FIRST TAKE THIS TEST.

HOW TO:
Read the sentences below. Decide if each one is true or false. To see if you are correct, check the answers on the opposite page.

QUESTIONS:

1. A school bus can enter someone's body and kids can go on a tour. True or false?

2. Museums are boring. True or false?

3. Arnold should not have tried to get back to school by himself. True or false?

4. Children cannot breathe or talk when they are surrounded by a liquid. True or false?

5. If the children really were as small as cells, we couldn't see them without a microscope. True or false?

6. White blood cells actually chase and destroy disease germs. True or false?

7. Ms Frizzle really knew where Arnold was the whole time. True or false?

ANSWERS:

1. False! That could not happen in real life. (Not even to Arnold.)

But in this story the author had to make it happen. Otherwise, the book would have been about a trip to a museum, instead of a trip through the body.

2. False! Museums are interesting and fun. But they are not as strange and gross as actually going inside a human body.

3. True! In real life, it would have been safer if Arnold had found a police officer to help.

4. True. If children were *really* inside a blood vessel, they would drown. It must have been magic.

5. True! The pictures in this book show the cells and the children greatly enlarged.

6. True! As unbelievable as it seems, real white blood cells actually behave just like the ones in this book. They even squeeze through the cells of blood vessel walls to capture germs in your organs and tissues.

7. Probably true. No one is absolutely sure, but most people think Ms Frizzle knows *everything*.

PLEASE DO NOT WRITE IN THIS BOOK.

THANK YOU.